A UNIQUE ECLECTIC
BOOK OF ESSAYS

JOHN JOSEPH MACK JR

PAGE PUBLISHING, INC.
New York, NY

First originally published by Page Publishing, Inc. 2015

ISBN 978-1-68213-071-1 (pbk)
ISBN 978-1-63417-928-7 (digital)
ISBN 978-1-68213-072-8 (hardcover)

Printed in the United States of America

CONTENTS

ACKNOWLEDGMENT

I also wish to acknowledge two lady librarians who not only helped me troubleshoot various ideas; supplied me with materials; especially for my paradigm/ diagrams but helped me maintain my inspirational drive to create. Thanks to Shirley Wayland and Cindy Herrington who together have helped to maintain a high quality library which is the Chapin Memorial Library in Myrtle Beach, SC. The Chapin Library has certainly been a lifesaver for me in my writing endeavors.

Wondering Space

I watch the stars in the midst of black
as they seem to stare directly back.

They glimmer and glitter throughout the
whole night.
The spatial expanse!
Oh, what a sight.

I wonder of life beyond man's touch…
Of tundras and canyons and jungles
as such.

If we are all alone in just our own
place,
then why all the clutter,
and why all the space?

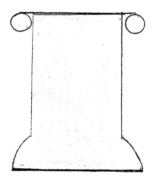

THE FORWARD VERSUS REVERSE MODES OF TIME TRAVEL AND PRESENT/PAST TIME

Considering time travel in forward and reverse modes, arrival to any future moment is achieved differently than in reverse-mode travel.

Forward-mode travel is expressed in Albert Einstein's variables of gravity and the speed-of-light constant. Arrival into a so-called future time utilizing these medium means would give the effect of traveling forward.

Due to the relative measurement and the intangible nature of time, it is still likely that a future time exists in essence as finite linear thinking has suggested. Future time is rather a future past moment that exists to be arrived at from the present which is in itself a fleeting past.

Hence, what should occur in the forward-travel mode is a delay on behalf of the traveling entity while confined within the medium means. This delay is reciprocal where the incremental duration from the perspective of the traveler is at a normal rate while the rate of the outside perspective it is seemingly accelerated.

Considering past time or simply the past as an imprint of moments onto an electromagnetic field, every occurrence that has ever happened is recorded within dimensions or upon a single spatial plane constituting a universe of records. Specifically, every microsecond moment or state of inertia is preserved in what is formed in dimensional regression where events are surreal in nature.

The act of physically traveling to the so-called past would involve a means of transcending space to the electromagnetic plane of existence. Entering a phantom universe would require finding or creating a warp in the electromagnetic spectrum whereby passage is possible. Time travel into the past would respectively fix the traveler into some past phantom era or encapsulate him within a surreal setting of illusionary images randomly strewn together in a collage matrix.

Implantation of a third party into a past time would have no affect upon changing the future, which might otherwise allow for the creation of a paradox. This reason being that the initial instance of actual happening, which is that past imprinted, is but a mere recorded image. A third party encapsulated within such a spatial continuum would be an unnoticed viewer who is part of the scene but without the ability to direct or influence a new course of action.

The overall hypothesis for both forward and reverse modes of time travel does not take into account the possible encounter a traveler might have within the space-time continuum with transplanted or passing spiritual energies such as ghosts, demons, or even God.

Multiple dimensionalities in the reality of past time would maintain time lines existing for as many variations of events from the present as is infinitely possible. Past time here exists as a series of phantom dimensions, each reciprocal to how events unfolded during present times.

Multiple dimensionalities in present time could mean more than one of the same being or thing existing throughout alternate lines. This idea stems from a theory that the universe inverts upon itself, mirroring all of existence once or indefinitely. This reasoning gives an illustration to what many men have wondered, namely, "Do I exist within another dimension as my same self better off or worse than I am now?" A multiplicity of time lines would offer resolution for solving the outcomes of the many fork-in-the-road event horizons confronting nature and living beings.

Only during the cascading present can time travel be initiated, going forward or backward. Time travel never existed in the past because it was never initiated then when the past was an unfolding present. If there was no time travel exercised in the past, then it can never be. Hence, time travel in the past is always an "into the past" arrived at from a future moment.

Multiple identical beings in various dimensions may initiate time travel or not, depending upon the different event horizons. In an electromagnetic/multidimensional juncture, a being may view its symmetrical other through the spatial plane. Union between two or more like or unlike beings could create a paradox for whatever time line is affected. A parallel being introduced within the same line, which precedes its other, may appear as a corporeal being or as that of a spiritual entity due to the effect of interspatial emergence. A similar explanation for this alludes to the vardoger phenomenon, which is defined as the projected being of a living being or person which precedes that being. Here again, both the projected being and the being it precedes are of the same dimension/continuum. And lastly to reason, one could never meet his other self in the future within the same dimension because the one traveling forward is the only one arriving into the future present.

Because present time passes in an instant before a conscious being is aware of the passing, it is impossible for a thinking being to realize present time.

A defining example of a present moment can be compared to a photograph or a single frame from film or video. The time it takes to record a single frame for television is a fraction of 1/32 of a second. A series of frame moments strung together show images in motion. Similarly, the real universe, or present time, unfolds, for a fraction of a second when it then recedes into a phantom state. Present time forever renews, continuing the forward/regress cycle.

Photographs or TV images, however, represent a pseudo phantom realm when compared to nature or living beings regressing into a phantom universe. That is because photographs and TV images are artificially reproduced from that of a real thing or being residing within a present moment. Such facsimiles are two-dimensional recreations with no separate states of consciousness. The conscious state that does exist is an illusion of consciousness, recorded, not free, and determined.

Consciousness or awareness must exist fully within a phantom universe because space and/or the electromagnetic spectrum encompasses everything, always including mental or spiritual energy. Once a real being becomes a living phantom, the conscious level is forever what it was when the total being was regressed into past time. Otherwise, the past could change similar to present time where first-chance event horizons await real beings. For example, a phantom being could invent a means of time travel with a new-found consciousness, changing the past or even affecting the present reality. This idea is contrary to the notion of imprinted things or consciousness.

In conclusion, time travel differs in the forward and reverse modes where forward travel is the result of delay utilizing Einstein's variable means. The past is a phantom universe to be arrived at by entering a time warp vis-à-vis the electromagnetic spectrum. The past can not be changed as it exists as a universe of record. Multidimensionality for past and present times would respectively maintain various time lines and beings. Like other beings are within their own astral plane and can be viewed through a time/dimension juncture but not met lest a paradox ensues.

Because the instance of time passage is so rapid, human perception of present time is virtually nonexistent. And although there are manmade examples of phantom states capturing a moment of inertia, such representations are pseudo images devoid of the consciousness that exists for phantom beings. The consciousness of phantom beings, however, remains what it was and cannot redirect new courses of events from the past.

A mortal undertaking such as time travel could never be a certainty when one also considers the intervention of extraterrestrial intelligence or the effects of passing alien spacecraft within the same corridors of space-time.

TIME LINE PARADIGM

TIME LINE PARADIGM

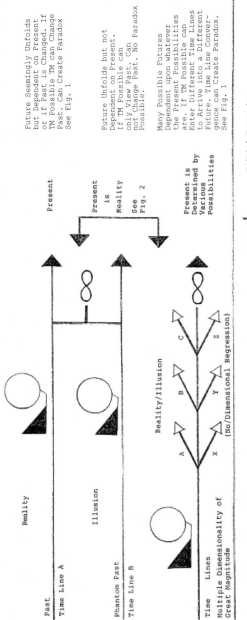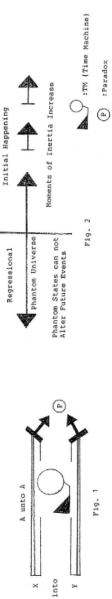

Reality

Past

Time Line A

Illusion

Phantom Past

Time Line B

Reality/Illusion

A B C

X Y Z

Time Lines

Multiple Dimensionality of
Great Magnitude

(No/Dimensional Regression)

Present

Present
is
Reality

See
Fig. 2

Present is
Determined by
Various
Possibilities

Future Seemingly Unfolds
but Dependent on Present
or if Past is Changed. If
TM Possible TM can Change
Past. Can Create Paradox
See Fig. 1

Future Unfolds but not
Dependent on Present.
If TM Possible can
only View Past. Can
not Change Past. No Paradox
Possible.

Many Possible Futures
Dependent upon whatever
the Present Possibilities
are. If TM Possible can
Enter Different Time Lines
to Arrive into a Different
Future. Time Line Conver-
gence can Create Paradox.
See Fig. 1

Regressional

Phantom Universe

Phantom States can not
Alter Future Events

Initial Happening

Moments of Inertia Increase

Fig. 2

↑ :TM (Time Machine)

Ⓟ :Paradox

A unto A

X

into

Y

Ⓟ

Fig. 1

FROZEN MOMENTS

Everything in the universe that happens has a moment of inertia. Inertia, as it pertains to inertness relating it to time, is an instant of time frozen. To reason, a value of time which is too fast to be measured is not time duration but, rather, a fixed instant during its elapse. In a given example, one quadrillionth of a millisecond is immeasurable. Such an instant is more likely to be time at rest during its stride as it continues on indefinitely. Hence, duration is a series of frozen time snippets that exist forever because they are frozen within the space continuum. This explanation compares to an effect of light speed, which states that anything or anyone attaining the speed of light will have the effect of stopped motion with time having ceased.

This notion of time on hiatus can be compared to a riddle of motion or distance covered. It reveals that all action must proceed from point A to point B. Upon travel, action must first distance itself halfway preceding that action halfway and so on (see illustration A). This paradox about movement concludes that motion should never begin, but things do move! It does however suffice to utilize the riddle/illustration in order to give an analogy in support for the argument over the inertness of motion which correlates with the notion of frozen time. So as the two are related, there is always a frozen moment of action and, thus, a frozen moment of time. And it is therefore inferred that when these snippets of time and motion are strewn together, there is the unfolding passage of time within the seemingly physical reality.

As this relates to the past, all moments of action in time to the present exist as reality (corporeal from within its own perspective but seen as memory from the perspective of a fleeting present). Hence, the civil war rages on, Benito Mussolini is in power in Italy, and America is celebrating its bicentennial in the year 1976. Oh, and a T. rex (*Tyrannosaurus rex*) is being gored somewhere back in the Cretaceous period by a triceratops.

Lastly, there are frozen moments in the future. For if the future can be prophesied or read, such as in the Bible code, Nostradamus's quatrains, or with déjà vu, it is something already remembered with its first instance of happening, and thus, it is that something that has already happened, being viewed from a past further back than the future moment—which is a present moment that has not passed yet—that is before what has passed before. Succinctly, if the future is remembered, it is only after it is bygone time.

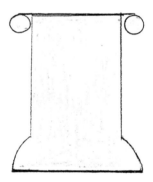

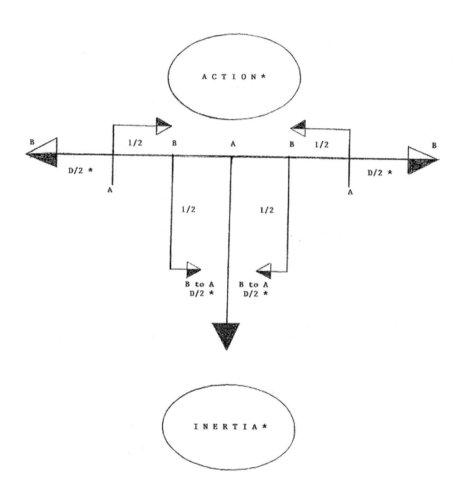

*Physical motion, A to B)
*D/2 – Distance halved, B to A
*Inertia – action/time frozen

Illustration A

TIME/DIMENSION PARADIGMS

TIME/DIMENSION PARADIGMS

<u>FUTURE</u>   <u>PRESENT</u>   <u>PAST</u>

      (REALITY)   NO/TIME

<u>FUTURE</u>   <u>PRESENT</u>   <u>PAST IS PHANTOM</u>

(Illusion/Reality)   <———|———>   Imprint
No/Time   (Illusion) No Time

<u>NO FUTURE</u>   <u>PRESENT ONLY</u>   <u>NO PAST</u>

                  NO TIME
          (REALITY) OR (ILLUSION)

<u>FUTURE</u>   <u>PRESENT</u>   <u>PAST</u>

      (ILLUSION)   NO/TIME

GOD IS NEVER EVERYWHERE

The ontological argument engaged here offers a rationalization to the improbability that an omnipotent God is a being that is omnipresent throughout the universe. As a theorem, it is not intended to acknowledge theism but, rather, to explore the physical limitations of a supernatural being's flight pattern throughout space if, indeed, such a being does exist.

Only nothing can exist everywhere throughout time. Space is infinite because it is nothingness. God who is infinite—unlike space but more so infinite than mortal beings—is limited in extension because its substance is something, namely, light/energy.

This limitation defines God as a being that, if he is to be somewhere, he must travel through space in order to encompass an area. It is an impossibility as well as a contradiction to imagine that God can be everywhere similar to the nonentity of space.

Again, only space can have an infinite expanse everywhere throughout time. Space is simply nothingness that exists everywhere where something doesn't exist. This rational truth must hold true within both the physical and metaphysical realms of reality because nothing remains nothing in either dimension.

God who is something has properties that must impose upon his entity an extension pattern of a relative sort, which is in and of itself finite when compared to space.

For example, no matter how fast God travels in any direction within an area, there is always that area that has yet to be journeyed across. Hence, there is always an area somewhere where he doesn't exist.

If a good God does exist, let mankind hope that Earth and its immediate surroundings are areas God has claimed, is claiming, or will claim.

SPACE

∞

A RATIONALE FOR SPACE

Space is nothingness in everywhere where there is nothing. It is the absence of something. If space were something, it would have to be something lesser than something true. But if that were true, how could something occupy the same place with space (a lesser something)? There would be no room for both somethings within the same place—as the true something needs its space to occupy!

Hence, if space is truly nothing, how can it fold or bend to create a wormhole? It cannot.

The idea exists in the minds of wishful astrophysicists and imaginative movie directors and writers. Do they not realize with their own eyes when they draw a lattice-drafted, horn-shaped wormhole upon an animated image showing examples of space folding or bending that they are applying physical formations and contours to nothing, which is nothing but empty space? Such believers must believe in magic!

If space is something, it had to have had a beginning. This idea is nonsense. If it had a beginning, then what existed before that—nothing but space?

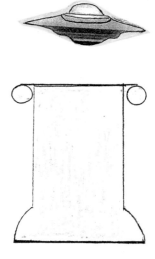

SOUL REINCARNATION

Considering reincarnation, many variations exist as to how a soul or spiritual energy can move through space and time. It is conceivable that a spirit can be transferred into a past that exists in either reality or in an illusion.

In the realm of reality, spiritual energy would pass into some past dimensional continuum where the future has yet to unfold.

In the case of an illusionary existence, a wandering soul would necessarily reincarnate as a kind of phantom being. And it is possible that the past exists as an electromagnetic phantom dimension imprinted in time and space similar to phantom images created by the electronic gun inside a television picture tube.

As far as reincarnation occurring from some present time into the future, it is likely only in the sense of a soul procrastinating its reentry, and whereafter, a spirit reembodiment occurs at whatever the present time is. Such procrastination on behalf of a spirit might account for the presence of seen or unseen ghosts.

The idea of linear time and linear dimensions must prevail in arguments for reincarnation because a soul will always reside in some before and after state in a past or present dimension if, indeed, souls do exist.

But would it also hold true if a soul reincarnated into the same person or creature over and over again to live the same life as it did before during exactly the same timespan where a soul becomes trapped in a single dimensional frame continuum?

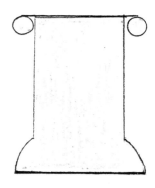

HUMAN RACE

Caucasoid, Mongoloid, and Negroid are the three racial groups that exist for *Homo sapiens* man according to anthropologists. The innate qualities of ethnic similarity inherent within each category are distinct and similar enough that there correlates qualities of dissimilarity between each of the racial groups mandating the natural biological separation of the human races.

These categorizations stem from mankind's evolvement down through the millennia to a point where mankind now exists as separate racial beings. It is the result of nature's experiment on a set of earthly creatures given particular environmental conditionings and subsequent human adaptations.

As racial categories exist then, so do they exist as maxims defining man into kinds, for it is racial being that ultimately gives definition and, therefore, meaning to human life.

It is given evidence that each kind dictates a genetical message-order whereby any given quality of similarity or likeness is to be maintained and thus perpetuated in a teleological sense to an end that is racial distinction of the very same. This innate communication is an overall natural exercise in sync with the biological truism that *Homo sapiens* are foremost creatures of distinct race. Conversely, it also dispels the biological notion of any biracial manifestation inasmuch as such human courses of action are antithetical to the outcome of race.

Emotionalism via the subjective traits of love and affection or the caring for another must always be secondary in behavioral action toward biological union because such human emotions come after the first constancy of race. Simply put, people must first maintain racial integrity, asserting affection, caring and/or love as means or ends thereafter.

FEMINISM VIA THE "BRAT–BITCH" SYNDROME

Feminism to me is a human characteristic that stems from an immature mindset inherent within the young female gender. When faddism, egocentricity, materialism, and self-centeredness erupt in the mind of a young girl and are not rectified through enlightened discourse or instruction, a young female will maintain and further develop attitudes that constrain, confuse, or muddle the acquisition of or the dispensation of a self-actualized state of being. Respectively, it would be as though such a female were stuck inside Plato's cave as either a seeker malforming ideas or as a quasi-intellectual who extols bits of knowledge while lacking in wisdom.

What develops from this uncorrected juvenile mental state is what I refer to as the brat-bitch syndrome.

Young women who develop this syndrome and maintain it as they continue through life become highly competitive and sensitive in their behavior, citing from a well of invalid or irrationalized reasoning.

And all too often these brat bitches enter learned institutions, first into high school and then to universities with their syndrome wrapped about them like a life preserver.

Of course, there are occasions when this delusionary/false-value state of mind is recognized for what it is and is cast at the wayside as further institutional or noninstitutional education is embraced. It is truly necessary that any methodology entered into for erudition is not ideologically skewed toward the liberal orthodoxy, secular materialism, or religious fanaticism. In the pursuit of wisdom, one must not only seek to leave Plato's cave but must also be instructed by those already outside the cave.

In the present era of the 1990s, it is all too apparent that women who envelope the brat-bitch syndrome and carry it forward coalesce their new-found intelligence within a matrix of falsehoods and faddist misinformation. It is clear that such a scenario can only create a human character that falls well short of something altruistic.

Now although boys have tendencies along the same lines that can be identified with the syndrome, males are or tend to be more analytical and less emotional in utilizing the sphere of the brain that accentuates the cognitive. This is a scientifically known fact.

It is the innateness of this factor in males that allows more readily for a conscious effort to reckon with or come to terms with the brat attitude.

It is obvious, of course, that there are exceptions. There are boys who never grow out of the syndrome and girls who do. My focus is, however, centered on girls who don't. It is the human female that tends to significantly perpetuate this emotional syndrome, brat bitch.

My concern is with the intellectual women of the day that suffer from this syndrome, and who hold important positions in government. They are people of influence in organizations that together contribute to affect public opinion and mold public policy affecting the culture climate.

In closing, I am particularly concerned with feminists who are so-called scholars and who are looked upon by other scholars as well as by students and the general public as great mentors. The delusion that exists here is a feminist scholar using her credentials like a cloak to hide her underlying self and purpose.

THE FALSEHOOD

OF

MALE

AND

FEMALE

The biological maxim for *Homo sapiens* is the heterosexual interplay between the genders of male and female. Whether a human being remains sexually celibate throughout an existence, engages in sex without procreating, or procreates offspring, all incidents are heterosexual by nature because *Homo sapiens* are heterosexual creatures. Homosexual/lesbian activity is truly a deviatory heterosexual interplay between like genders.

Like-gender sexual activity is human behavior as such where mental stimulus is coerced into varied abnormal modes vis-à-vis whatever idiosyncrasy prevails to incite participation. It becomes action where people engage in heterosexual interplay while denying the very concept that allows it to be possible. Delusions are created where something new is invented, and that something new has validity as something in and of itself. To give an analogy: It is like understanding the idea of hammering a nail while utilizing either two hammers or two nails to follow through with the idea of what is intended for a hammer and nail. Certainly one can try to hammer a hammer like a nail or use a nail like a hammer to hammer another nail, giving validity to both actions. It is clear, however, that either action is erroneous when only the obvious will suffice.

As a concept, homosexuality/lesbianism is inherently a contradiction and is thus null and void as to having validity. Heterosexuality is the only valid axiom in sync with the biological nature of mankind. Both concepts can be compared given concepts A and B.

Concept A (heterosexuality) stands alone as a truth without relying upon criterion from concept B (homosexuality). The existence of mankind proves concept A to be the only valid biological axiom.

However, concept B must rely upon criterion from concept A in order to exist while simultaneously manifested as a notion antithetical to what it borrows from. Hence, such a concept is hypocritical and is a contradiction. It is a true misconception.

As for information variables, ill faddist cultures, societal misinterpretations, and misconstructions have and continue to cause the many misconceptions of civilized man. The specific erroneous concept of homosexuality/lesbianism is primarily the outcome of environmental conditioning where such information variables instruct to influence deviatory sexual misbehavior, allowing for the manifestation of falsehoods, namely that of perverse physical interactions and that of perverse attitudes toward sexual conduct. As for specific emotions such as love and affection, they are made false in homosexual/lesbian affairs through misapplication.

The misapplication of emotion is an inherent error where turnabout from proper application is the result of mental delusion stemming from environmental misdirection or biological dysfunction that perpetuates the falsehood of like-gender mismatching.

In heterosexual affairs, the emotional application of love and affection with sexual interaction utilized as either means or as ends is in sync with biological functions. Such expressions of love and affection vis-à-vis any sexual exchange is, of course, natural and correct.

Where sexual interaction is not a factor, love and affection take on a different connotation and can certainly be expressed or directed to the like gender as in friendship or as with progeny and siblings.

Overall, homosexual/lesbian dispositions that arise as falsehoods are not only out-of-sync with biology but exist to further corrupt opposite-gender interaction within a society.

It is befitting, in closing, to characterize those people of the sort who willfully brand upon themselves the homosexual or lesbian labels as types of naïve creatures who stray from nature and whose sense of altruism and reason have become something vile.

THE MACK CANON

When the plot of a story in film or television becomes farfetched whereby logic is stretched to the limit, the contrivance calls attention to itself as something predetermined and thus unrealistic.

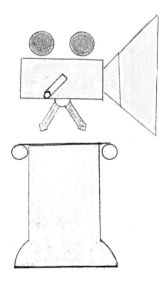